THE SCOOP ON POOP

POOP Power

by Ellen Lawrence

Consultant:
Garret Suen, Assistant Professor
Department of Bacteriology
University of Wisconsin
Madison, Wisconsin

BEARPORT
PUBLISHING

New York, New York

Credits

Cover, © John Bracegirdle/Alamy, © Anubhab Roy/Shutterstock, and © OlegD/Shutterstock; 4T, © AuntSpray/Shutterstock; 4B, © Nigel Bean/Nature Picture Library; 5, © Christian Jegou Publiphoto Diffusion/Science Photo Library; 6, © Fotosearch/Getty Images; 7TL, © Greentellect Studio/Shutterstock; 7, © Mauro Toccaceli/Alamy; 8L, © Ruth Owen; 8R, © Ghislain Cottat/Creative Commons; 9, © M. Burgess/Classic Stock/Alamy; 10, © Aleksander Hunta/Shutterstock; 11, © Bjorn Svensson/Alamy; 12, © Ashley Cooper Pics/Alamy; 13, © Design Pics Inc/Alamy and © smereka/Shutterstock; 14, © Vladimir Wrangel/Shutterstock; 15, © Ruby Tuesday Books; 16, © Loowatt Ltd.; 17, © Loowatt Ltd.; 18T, © Milkovasa/Shutterstock; 18B, © Tian Gan/Shutterstock; 19, © Shotshop GmbH/Alamy; 20T, © Evan Lorne/Shutterstock; 20B, © Justin Kase ztwoz/Alamy; 21, © Sikarin Supphatada/Shutterstock; 22, © Tapilipa/Shutterstock; 23TL, © Evan Lorne/Shutterstock; 23TC, © Ashley Cooper Pics/Alamy; 23TR, © Sciencepics/Shutterstock; 23BL, © viki2win/Shutterstock; 23BC, © Christian Jegou Publiphoto Diffusion/Science Photo Library; 23BR, © pingphuket/Shutterstock.

Publisher: Kenn Goin
Editor: Jessica Rudolph
Creative Director: Spencer Brinker
Photo Researcher: Ruth Owen Books

Library of Congress Cataloging-in-Publication Data

Names: Lawrence, Ellen, 1967– author.
Title: Poop power / by Ellen Lawrence.
Description: New York, New York : Bearport Publishing, [2018] | Series: The
  scoop on poop | Audience: Ages 5–8. | Includes bibliographical references
  and index.
Identifiers: LCCN 2017016596 (print) | LCCN 2017025658 (ebook) |
ISBN 9781684023004 (Ebook) | ISBN 9781684022465 (library)
Subjects: LCSH: Renewable energy sources—Juvenile literature. | Animal
  droppings—Juvenile literature. | Feces—Juvenile literature. | Power
  resources—Juvenile literature.
Classification: LCC TJ808.2 (ebook) | LCC TJ808.2 .L39 2018 (print) | DDC
  333.79/4—dc23
LC record available at https://lccn.loc.gov/2017016596

For more information, write to Bearport Publishing Company, Inc., 45 West 21st Street, Suite 3B, New York, New York 10010. Printed in the United States of America.

10 9 8 7 6 5 4 3 2 1

Contents

Prehistoric Poop Power

A pile of stinky poop might seem useless and yucky.

However, poop can actually be very useful—as **fuel**!

For thousands of years, **prehistoric** people used wood, dead leaves, and animal bones to build fires.

Yet they also collected lumps of dried dung from animals, such as woolly mammoths, to burn as fuel.

an illustration of woolly mammoths

mammoth dung

4

Prehistoric people made fires for warmth, light, cooking, and to scare wild animals away from their camps.

Fuel From Buffaloes

Animal dung was especially useful to people who lived in places where there were few trees.

The Great Plains is an area of flat, grassy land in North America.

Native Americans who lived there long ago burned dried buffalo dung.

They also hunted buffaloes for their meat, and used their skins to make tents and clothes.

When European settlers came to the Great Plains in the 1800s, they used buffalo dung as fuel, too. They called the round, flat lumps of dry poop "buffalo chips."

a settler gathering buffalo chips

Burning Beans

There are also few trees in the Andes Mountains in South America.

For hundreds of years, people in Peru have been burning llama droppings for cooking and heating.

People also spread the animal's poop on fields to help their crops grow.

The droppings, known as beans, are easy to collect.

That's because a herd of llamas often poops in one spot!

In the 1800s, people traveled by steamship on Lake Titicaca in the Andes. There was no wood, coal, or oil in the mountains to fuel the ship's engines. Instead, the steamship was powered by llama beans.

llama beans

the poop-powered ship

a Peruvian girl with a llama

Burning dung makes sense if there is no wood around. Why else might burning poop be a good idea?

Why Burn Dung?

Today, many people around the world burn the dung of the animals they raise.

Why is this a good idea?

Burning dung helps keep the land clean and free of germs that can harm people.

Poop fuel also costs nothing, so it saves people money.

Animals such as cows and yaks produce lots of poop—the supply never runs out!

a yak

In order to burn wood, people must cut down trees. Burning dung helps save trees.

These people in China are collecting yak dung.

Rotting Poop

Animal waste isn't only used as fuel for fires.

It can also be used to make gas and electricity. How?

On a farm, animal dung is collected and put into a huge tank called a biodigester.

Inside the tank, the poop starts to rot.

As the poop breaks down, **biogas** is released into the tank.

Inside your **digestive system**, tiny living things called bacteria break down food. This produces gas, which sometimes escapes from your body as a fart. This happens inside a biodigester, too. Bacteria break down poop and make gas.

biodigester

How do you think biogas is turned into electricity?

cow dung mixed with straw

13

Gas and Electricity

The gas in the biodigester tank floats into a large container, or holder.

Then pipes carry some of the gas from the holder into the farmhouse.

Here, it's burned to power the stove.

The rest of the gas goes into a machine called a generator.

The generator burns the gas and turns it into electricity.

It's not only farm dung that can be turned into poop power. At the Toronto Zoo in Canada, zoo poo from rhinos, giraffes, and many other animals will be used to make electricity in a biodigester.

How a Biodigester Works

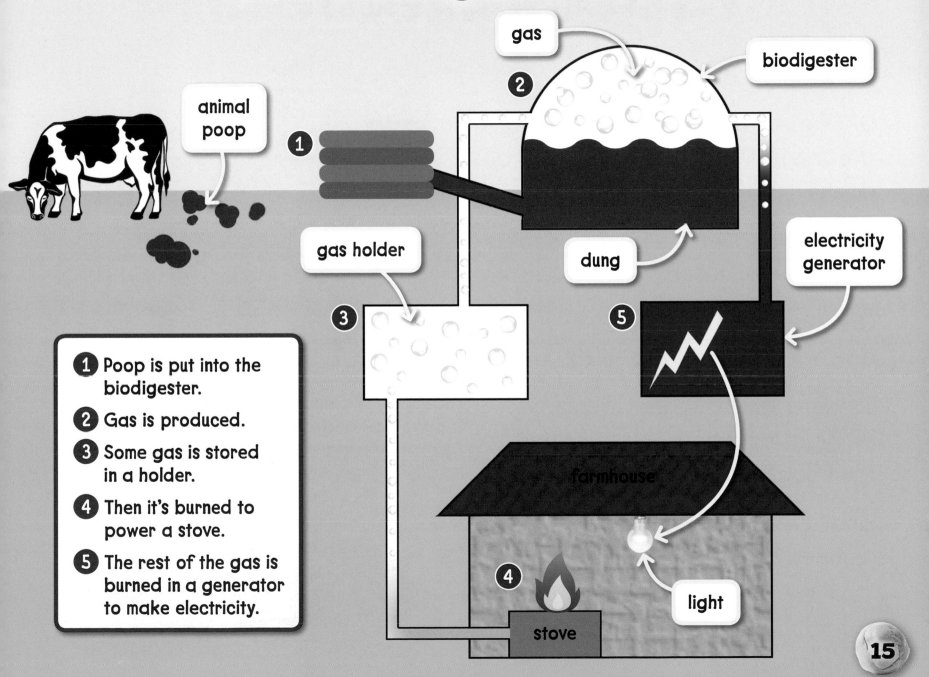

gas

biodigester

②

animal poop

① biodigester

gas holder

dung

electricity generator

③ gas holder

⑤

1 Poop is put into the biodigester.

2 Gas is produced.

3 Some gas is stored in a holder.

4 Then it's burned to power a stove.

5 The rest of the gas is burned in a generator to make electricity.

farmhouse

light

④

stove

Special Toilets

Did you know there's a special toilet that can turn urine and poop into power?

Inside the toilet is a **biodegradable** bag that collects a person's waste.

Once a person is done using the restroom, the toilet seals the bag.

Workers take the bags to a biodigester, where the bags and their contents rot and make gas.

Finally, the gas is burned in a generator to make electricity!

The toilet is made by a company called Loowatt.

bag

cell phones charging with poop-powered electricity

In Madagascar in Africa, many people do not have toilets or electricity. Loowatt is helping people there build the toilets that turn poop into gas and electricity.

Flushed Away

Usually, when a person uses the toilet, the **sewage** is flushed away.

The waste flows through huge underground pipes to a sewage plant.

There, the dirty water is cleaned.

Then the clean water is pumped into rivers or the ocean.

The poopy, leftover stuff is known as sewage sludge.

Is it possible to do something useful with this waste?

Waste gets flushed down a toilet.

sewage in a cleaning pool at a sewage plant

Sewage sludge is normally taken to a landfill. Then it's buried in the ground along with the garbage that's collected from homes and businesses.

sewage sludge

How do you think sewage sludge could be turned into fuel?

The Future Is Poo!

At a special plant, sewage sludge is mixed with other biodegradable waste such as food scraps.

The mixture is heated until it becomes thick and black.

Then all the liquid is removed, leaving a powder.

Finally, the powder is made into small lumps, or pellets, that can be burned like coal.

This may be more high-tech than in prehistoric times, but it's still poop power!

food scraps

pellets for burning

In Japan, scientists are making hydrogen gas from sewage sludge. They're using the gas as fuel for cars designed to run on hydrogen. One day, you may drive a car that's powered by poop!

a hydrogen-powered car

TOYOTA

MIRAI

Science Lab

Be a Poop Fuel Inventor

Discover a new type of fuel that's made from a plant-eating animal's poop. Draw a poster that tells people all about your new poop fuel. First, do some research online, and then think about the answers to these questions:

What animal produces the poop?

How will the poop be used? For example, is it dried and burned? Is the poop made into something else, such as a liquid, like oil, for burning?

What is your new poop fuel called?

Why is it a good idea for people to use your poop fuel?

You will need:
- A large sheet of paper
- Colored pencils or markers

Jumbo Fuel
Made by Elephants

New Jumbo fuel is dried in the Sun.

Elephant dung contains lots of dried plant material that burns well.

An elephant produces more than 100 pounds (45 kg) of dung each day. Clean up the zoo by burning the poo.

Burn poop instead of cutting down trees!

Science Words

biodegradable (*bye*-oh-di-GRAY-duh-buhl) something that rots or breaks down naturally

biogas (BYE-oh-gass) gases from rotting waste that can be used as fuel

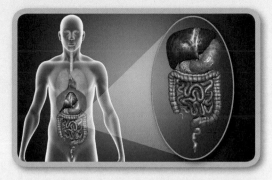

digestive system (dye-JESS-tiv SISS-tuhm) the stomach and other organs in a body that break down food

fuel (FYOO-uhl) materials such as coal, oil, or wood that are burned to produce heat or power

prehistoric (pree-hi-STORE-ik) a time, thousands of years ago, when people did not keep written records of their lives and history

sewage (SOO-ij) liquid and solid waste that is flushed down toilets

Index

Read More

Cooley Peterson, Megan. *How Water Gets from Treatment Plants to Toilet Bowls (Pebble Plus).* Mankato, MN: Capstone (2016).

Weakland, Mark. *Onion Juice, Poop, and Other Surprising Sources of Alternative Energy.* Mankato, MN: Capstone (2011).

Woolf, Alex. *You Wouldn't Want to Live Without Poop!* New York: Scholastic (2016).

Learn More Online

To learn more about poop power, visit **www.bearportpublishing.com/TheScoopOnPoop**

About the Author

Ellen Lawrence lives in the United Kingdom. Her favorite books to write are those about nature and animals. In fact, the first book Ellen bought for herself, when she was six years old, was the story of a gorilla named Patty Cake that was born in New York's Central Park Zoo.

Answer to Page 7

A buffalo eats mostly grass. As the grass passes through the animal's body, the tough fibers in the grass don't break down, so the poop contains lots of grassy material. Once the dung dries, it burns well, just like dry grass.